PeopleTek

Creating Successful Leaders.

PeopleTek's   Leadership Journey II

PeopleTek's **Leadership Journey II**

Moving Beyond The Barriers

Michael W. Kublin

authorHOUSE®

AuthorHouse™ LLC
1663 Liberty Drive
Bloomington, IN 47403
www.authorhouse.com
Phone: 1-800-839-8640

Published by AuthorHouse   03/19/2014

ISBN: 978-1-4918-7203-1 (sc)
ISBN: 978-1-4918-7202-4 (e)

Library of Congress Control Number: 2014904813

Contents

Dedicated to my PeopleTek Team:
Helenne Deutscher, Jan Mayer-Rodriguez, and Pat Pinera
for making Leadership Journey II a reality!

From The Author

Exclusively for Leadership Journey I graduates, *Journey II—Moving Beyond The Barriers*, is a professional development program focused on the application of leadership business concepts and the creation of comprehensive individual action plans that support skill development and strategies for organizational improvement.

Journey II is dedicated to assessing what you as an individual desire to change and implement. For example, what's required to achieve your business goals? To clarify and live your role? To support your organization's success?

You will formulate new strategies and behaviors to strengthen and sustain your leadership skills by understanding how to:

- Achieve and manage WORK EXPECTATIONS
- Manage CHANGE while supporting your vision and organizational goals
- Develop TRUST within yourself and others
- Learn to INFLUENCE positively and with authority
- Implement COPING and STRESS mechanisms
- MASTER TIME by eliminating the detractors that impede results

Eliminate barriers that get in the way of achieving the results you desire; I wish you a successful and an enlightening Journey!

Sincerely,
Mike

Session 1—Introduction

Welcome to PeopleTek's
Leadership Journey® II—Moving Beyond the Barriers!

In this program you will be learning about and experiencing a leadership effectiveness improvement process. Leadership development requires that you try various processes to be effective and authentic in your own way.

You will be guided through a series of self discoveries that hold the secret for improving your leadership behaviors, techniques and processes. You will learn tools that you can immediately apply to the work you are doing today.

To help you do that, we will be working together over a period of time so that we may introduce the tools, put them into practice, and then discuss the results you are experiencing. You will become aware of what is happening to you in your career as a leader, what you want to accomplish and what is getting in your way.

We ask you to keep a learning journal, a Leadership Travel Journal, to document your experience. Please take notes on what you are thinking, feeling and doing as this *Journey* is traveled together!

During the sessions you will continue your Leadership Journey and build on your leadership skills and abilities already acquired. We will also focus on those barriers that are getting in the way of success, and detracting from achieving your Vision, Mission and Goals.

The first thing that we need to do is make certain that we have all of the tools that we need to ensure our success. We will assess where our advanced journey is going, how we're going to get there, and even look for possible destinations.

The second step is committing to the Journey and increasing our awareness of our leadership skills. This includes having a safe place to store the treasures that we find along the way.

Next we will want to remember (and record) all important points of interest (ex. any "a-ha's", "oops", or things you just don't want to lose sight of).

The final and most important aspect of this journey is our willingness to understand and possibly change our actions.

WORKSHOP GOALS:

What should you expect to get out of PeopleTek's *Leadership Journey® II* program? When it's completed, you will have:

- An increased awareness of leadership skills, abilities and behaviors that will allow you to be more successful.
- Identified barriers that are getting in the way of success and develop skills, abilities and behaviors that will best advance your leadership capabilities.
- Learned new tools and processes that can be used at any time during your leadership career.
- Learned how to effectively deal with others and how to utilize their unique skills and abilities.
- Be clear about your individual leadership essence/vision and how you can continue to leverage it.
- Utilize the **Leadership Journey**™ **II** to supplement what you ultimately want to create and achieve.
- Understand how the new leadership tools will help you continue to grow and better relate to others.

Course Objectives:

1. Learn the ground rules of the program.
2. Maximize our environment so that we can function at our full potential.
3. Learn how effective we are at communicating with others and ourselves.
4. Assess our influencing style and determine its rate of success.
5. Control our most limited resource—time.
6. Determine if stress motivates you or debilitates you.
7. Enable you to control your responses to your environment.
8. Increase your flexibility.
9. Identify the barriers that are getting in the way of success; i.e. find out if and where you are stuck.

<u>Reminder:</u> **Leadership is the ability to influence an individual or group to achieve specific goals and take them where they've never gone before and wouldn't go by themselves.**

Let's begin!

When we take a journey we need to have a vehicle. Let's say you are the vehicle for this journey. There are bumps and ruts along the way and not all of the roads are smooth. Some roads are uphill and it takes a lot of gas (energy) to go a short distance; some of the roads go down hill and we get where we want to be in a relatively short time.

As we continue our advanced *Journey* we need to be prepared for any eventuality. A wise traveler is well prepared so if anything goes awry they will be able to respond to and resolve the situation, or at least be equipped to get help.

It is the intention of this course to give you the tools you require to assist you in your travels through life. You're not going to get all the answers, but you will receive the tool kit that will help you address breakdowns that may occur along the way.

Sometimes, we feel as though we have put ourselves in a box without any windows or doors; this program is going to provide you with some windows and doors. The most limiting feelings are those of feeling powerless and hopeless. We will minimize those feelings and remind you that options do exist, and that you have choices.

As with all PeopleTek programs, you are requested to keep a learning journal . . . a *Leadership Travel Journal,* to document your experiences. Please take notes on what you are thinking, feeling and doing as you progress on your *Journey.*

Ice Breaker—Sharing "You"

1. Why are you interested in Leadership Journey II?

2. What do you want to achieve for yourself?

3. What is the one thing you would like to change in your work life balance?

4. What gives you joy?

5. What is one thing you dislike about your job?

6. If you could re-live your life what (if anything) would you change?

Exercise 1.1—More About You

Note: Provide answers that you will be willing to share with the class

1. What is something about you that you would like others to know?

2. What is the one aspect of yourself that you like the most?

3. What is the one aspect of yourself that you would change?

4. List 3 goals at work that are a priority for you. (short term 6 months or less)

    - _____
    - _____
    - _____

5. List 3 long range goals you would like to achieve in 2+ years.

    - _____
    - _____
    - _____

6. List 3 actions you would need to do to achieve your short range goals and 3 actions for your long range goals.

    - (SHORT RANGE)_____ _____ _____
    - (LONG RANGE) _____ _____ _____

Exercise 1.2—Where Are You Now?

On a scale of 1-6, please rate yourself and your present skill level. (1 is the least; 6 almost perfect)

RATING

1. You adapt to change quickly and always look for new benefits.   _____
   List any ideas you have to improve your rating:

2. Evaluate your communication skills.   _____
   List any ideas you have to improve your rating:

3. How would you rate your ability to influence and negotiate with others?   _____
   List any ideas you have to improve your rating:

4. You use stress as a motivator for you (versus a debilitator)   _____
   List any ideas you have to improve your rating:

5. You effectively manage your time   _____
   List any ideas you have to improve your rating:

Your highest score: _____ Your lowest score _____

Self-Talk—Lessons To Learn

The way we talk to ourselves affects how we feel and what we do. We can talk to ourselves by telling ourselves things inside our heads. This is called **covert self-talk**.

There are three ways that we talk to ourselves. They are:

1) negative self talk
2) neutral self-talk
3) positive self-talk

Our self-talk determines our actions. In fact, you might say that it creates our reality. Because our schedules are so busy and we're usually multi-tasking, we don't take the time to bother listening to what it is we are saying to ourselves.

That is our biggest mistake. The demands of our day to day activities can overwhelm us if we are not vigilant about what we are saying to ourselves. Reality is created from the inside out; it is not created from the outside in. A favorite saying is:

"If you don't like your life, change your thoughts".

Think about this for a minute. Your life can become whatever it is that you think it is. If you talk to yourself in the "I can" and "I will" mode, you will find that "you can" and "you will".

Have you ever experienced being in a great mood and then you came upon a group who were talking negatively and you suddenly found yourself also feeling the negativity? It all started when your self talk shifted and was reinforced by the other people. Negative self talk impacts your interpersonal relationships, how you communicate, your stress levels, how you influence people and how you manage change.

What could you do when the environment is out of your control and everyone seems to be talking about rumors of change without anyone knowing exactly what is going to change? It is easy to say "be positive" in your self talk, but it is sometimes very difficult to do.

This is where your level of commitment comes in. If you have committed to yourself the willingness to change your behaviors this is the perfect time to begin. The challenge of dedication and determination are when opportunities arise that allow us to see where it is we really are, and what it is that we are willing to do. With greater challenges, there are increased opportunities for growth and dedication!

Ask yourself: "Am I willing to do whatever it takes to make me feel good?" If you think you are worth it, this is called self esteem.

SELF ESTEEM

Self esteem is the meter in which we measure our choices. Everything in life is a choice and we are constantly choosing. When we think we are worthy of feeling good our choices will reflect that, and when we think we deserve to be punished our choices will reflect that as well.

We are our own mirror and we have the power to shape our lives on the inside. Life and its circumstances are out of our control, yet we can control the most powerful tool we have which is our thoughts. Life becomes whatever it is you think it is. If you think your life is good it will be good no matter what is happening or not happening on the outside. If you think your life is garbage it will become garbage for you no matter how many wonderful things are happening for you.

Think of the old adage which states either "my cup is half full" or "my cup is half empty". It is your choice but it has been said that people who see their lives as a gift experience mental stability, health, and an attitude that encourages people to want to be in their presence. Those that have the opposite view often times find themselves alone because they are no fun to be around. (They don't want to be around themselves either, but they are stuck with themselves!)

Exercise 1.3—Self talk; positive or negative?

1. Do you consider yourself to be a positive or negative thinker and person? Why?

2. Do you listen to your self-talk? Give an example

3. In personal awareness do you think that others perceive you as you are or do they see you differently? Think of an example.

4. Are you a good negotiator or do you give in easily and feel it is easier to "go with the flow" instead of standing firm for what you want?

5. Are your behaviors predictable or are they different according to a given situation?

6. Are you a different person at work than when you are at home? Give examples.

Session 2—Work Expectations

Objectives

1. Learn what expectations you have as to what will happen in your career now and in the future.
2. Determine how these expectations may influence your attitude.
3. Discover which expectations are most important to you.
4. Increase your job satisfaction level.

Expectations and Intentions

What is an expectation and how does it affect us, our relationships, and our career? According to Webster's dictionary the definition is "the degree of probability that something will occur".

We all have expectations and another word for it might be result. Every action that we do brings with it a result. Sometimes we are aware of the result and sometimes we are not. We do something and the result (or consequence) comes back home to us whether we like it or not. The world is unpredictable and so are our actions and the actions of others. Unfortunately, there are no guarantees in life and sometimes what we do brings unexpected results and consequences.

Intention is another word that can be used along with expectation. They both impact the same thing: the RESULT. Whatever our actions, we expect certain results. Sometimes actions that we have used in the past have brought desirable results. Other actions have resulted in a non-positive outcome yet we keep doing them hoping that the negative result will become positive. *Why do we keep doing the same thing and expect a different result?*

Getting stuck often occurs when we are caught up in a habit. We have done it that way and we will continue it even if it causes us pain and suffering. That thought is called being in a comfort zone; we are used to it and we like the "known". The thought of leaving it and going out into the unknown is so frightening to us that we often choose to stay there just because it is so familiar to us.

Sometimes we hold unreal expectations for ourselves, our jobs and our relationships. It is difficult for us to know if they are real or unreal. If they are real there is a great opportunity for us to succeed and achieve the results we are hoping for. If it is unreal then we are merely setting ourselves up for disappointment because the chances of success are minimal.

This works on the same principle as goals. How many times have we set ourselves up by giving ourselves unrealistic goals? Who did that? The answer is clear; we did! And the same holds true for expectations.

Unrealized Expectations

Have you ever been involved in a relationship and expected them to know what you needed and wanted from them? Most of the time it didn't happen and we called this unrealized expectations. Then we became angry and expressed "if you loved me you should know". Well, they should not know if you didn't specifically tell them. Never assume that your expectations are known.

It is the same with job expectations. Why should your boss reward you for all of your contributions and hours of diligence for getting the job done if you never told them the value you provided and how many hours you did put in? You expected him/her to know, and when your expectations were not met you felt anger and resentment. There is no guarantee to result, but you can take responsibility for doing all you can to get the result you desire.

EXERCISE 2.1—(UN) Fulfilled Expectations

1. Write about a recent experience when your expectations were either fulfilled or unfulfilled.

2. Were your expectations realistic? How do you know?

3. What goals have you set to guarantee your success?

4. Write about one action that you feel you did or did not do that directly affected your desired outcome.

5. What could you have done differently to help you achieve your desired outcome?

EXERCISE 2.2—Expectations Further Examined

Circle 5 words below that are important to you in the achievement of your work expectations. (Add other key words if not listed).

Organization	Communication	Autonomy
Results	Recognition	Environment
Structure	Teamwork	Reward/recognition
Commitment	Diversity	Goals
Focus	Balance	Intention
Leader	Peers	Business Partners

Others:

After you have circled these elements list the top three in the order of importance to you in the achievement of your expectations.

1.

2.

3.

- Explain choice #1; how do you leverage this to get your desired results?

- Explain choice #2: how do you leverage this to get your desired results?

- Explain choice #3; how do you leverage this to get your desired results?

Focus

Focus is a word that is continually used in the work place, yet few understand what focus is or how to use it effectively

When focus is used correctly, it is an opportunity for you to create the results you desire. There are so many diverse ways that focus is used and in the work place of today it is almost impossible to stay focused on only one thing.

Focus is one of the most important elements of achievement because it is what drives us to the result. Without it we become scattered, unorganized, and pulled in so many directions that sometimes our desired end results are a blur and therefore not achieved.

To understand fully the impact of focus we must understand what it is. Focus is a laser beam. The intensity of the laser is encased in a small beam of light. That is what makes it so powerful. The broader the beam of light becomes, the weaker it becomes.

When our thoughts are consistent, they gain energy and intensity. In other words, the more we think about that same thought, the stronger our focus becomes and it manifests itself accordingly. We create what we give energy to! The more diluted the focus, the less chance of creating it.

Have you ever had the experience of creating your own worst fear? You did it by focusing on it. The more focus you give it, the quicker and stronger it becomes. Change your thoughts and you will change your life. THOUGHTS CREATE!

Understanding focus is the key to the achievement of success. It carries us past the "I can't" straight to the "I can and will". The glue that holds focus together is our thoughts, our intentions, and our self-talk. Thoughts create our reality and it is of great importance that we monitor and become vigilant about what we are thinking and saying to ourselves.

Awareness is everything. Intention precedes actions; at times we are aware of our intentions, and sometimes we are not. Intention is based upon the results we want. What happens when we get the results we didn't want? How do we find out our true intention? Do the results validate what we truly intended? Key questions to ask:

- Are my goals achievable?
- Did I set a realistic timeframe?
- Am I setting myself up (and/or my team) for failure?
- Did I take responsibility for my actions and how much did my actions impact the results (either positively or negatively)?
- Did circumstances occur that were out of my control and impact the results?

Actions and Results

We also need to objectively look at what we are doing, our self-talk, and assess whether our actions are in alignment and taking us towards our goals.

If it is not taking you where you would like to go, stop doing it and begin to put in new actions immediately. Again, if the result that you want is not happening, stop using that action!

This class is dealing with specific expectations of work. If your expectations are not being met, this is the time to examine those expectations closely. Begin to measure how close or distant these expectations are for you, and if you have or have not used reality (not what you want it to be, what it actually is) in choosing these goals. Your level of satisfaction is directly attained by the distance you are from your expectations.

Many times we choose a position on status, on salary, or because it's a promotion. We don't think it through thoroughly. It is important to look at the position closely and definitively. Not what you want it to be, but exactly what it is. Clearly defining for yourself what is expected of you, and whether you are willing to meet those expectations will impact your level of satisfaction and fulfillment.

If you have considerable doubt, consider not taking the position. If you do take it, in a short period of time you may be angry, resentful and frustrated. Job satisfaction directly affects your work performance. Unhappy workers have lower performance ratings, produce less, and their attitudes render them unapproachable.

Approachability in the workplace is one of the most important aspects of job performance. It directly impacts communications. It will also directly impact team performance as well as your own performance. Cooperation is a key factor when a worker is being evaluated and is closely associated with being approachable.

Have you ever had the experience of approaching a leader or co-worker who put up barriers, appeared distant, or quite frankly would not communicate with you? Chances are you went out of your way to avoid future dealings with that individual even if it meant not getting the information you needed to complete your task. People would rather take a risk for not getting everything they needed if it meant having to deal with "that one".

What can you do to increase work expectations and satisfaction?

The answer is clear and simple, doing it is another matter. If you find yourself in a position that feels like a dead end for you, your job satisfaction will be impacted. You will have feelings of dissatisfaction and feel that you are a victim. Instead of feeling miserable and victimized, you can change your thoughts and the results by aligning your actions to better support your goals and ultimate success.

You may wish to seek another position within the company (if this is an option) or you may have to consider seeking employment elsewhere.

These are risks, but it is a much higher risk factor for you to keep doing what is not working for you. Levels of stress are greatly impacted by job satisfaction, and over the long range your health will begin to suffer as your level of stress increases.

EXERCISE 2.3—Job Satisfaction

1. Briefly describe a job in which your expectations were not being fulfilled:

2. How did you feel about having to go to work every day?

3. How did it affect your work productivity?

4. Did you feel as though you were trapped?

5. What was the result? Are you still in the position? If yes, what are you doing to make it better for yourself? If the answer is no, how did it get resolved, and are you happier now?

Session 3—Time Mastery

Objectives

1. Learn where your strengths and weakness are in managing time.
2. Identify the habits that you want to change and craft out new ones.
3. Create a personalized action plan; define strategies that will improve your time management skills.
4. Adopt behaviors which increase your understanding of priorities, delegation and new behaviors.

Why we are here?

Time mastery is a problem that the work force is continually dealing with. There just never seems to be enough time. Through the years the push has been to produce more work with fewer resources. There seems to be an avalanche of work with not enough time to do it.

Time is a commodity that is in short supply. We are a goal driven society and achievement of our goals benefits us both professionally and personally. It seems as though setting goals for ourselves is easy; the catch is, can we achieve them? If we set goals for ourselves and do not commit the time to accomplish them, we are going to not feel good about ourselves and have a sense of failure. Ask yourself "what can I do about it and how can I do better"?

This session is going to enable you to begin to better deal with your work life balance. It may not be the total answer, but it will provide guidance. Remember, you are the one who will be in charge of what you do with the information that is presented to you today

Situation:

With so much work to do and not enough time to do it, the sense of being overwhelmed is experienced. This impacts productivity and our sense of accomplishment. One way to overcome this is to stay "in the now", the moment, the day. In order to do that one must be focused with each goal a priority. There is so much information in that one sentence; let's break it apart and take it one piece at a time.

When we feel as though we are drowning in a sea of work, and more is continually being asked of us, our level of stress increases and our coping mechanisms drop significantly.

We are sometimes assured that "it is alright if you say no, I will understand if your plate is full and there will be no consequences for you". Yet we frequently get pushback with the response "I know you can do it, I have confidence in you, I know you will do a great job as usual."

In the leader's mind, they feel they have given the person the opportunity to say no, but in truth did the person actually hear that or did they hear something totally different? If you think that most individuals end up taking on the new task you are absolutely correct.

The level of stress experienced increases considerably and coping mechanisms rapidly fall. The road to burnout is near and once on it, the escalation is very rapid; productivity suffers and creativity is shutting down. We are constantly reading about reductions in the work force and that we live in an instant world. Our clients, customers and leaders expect immediate responses to their requests, their voice messages, and their e-mails. Don't you?

We all want instant results. Managers want skills to be developed, and they say they want the training which used to take three days to be completed in three hours. (Joanne Sujansky, founder and CEO Keygroup Consulting)

The world of technology has made people more accessible and processes have been accelerated. Therefore, workers are expected to be available 24/7. The result is that employees are working longer and harder and levels of stress heightened.

Heated competition and increased customer demands are sources of aggravated stress.

The use of technology has promoted a lack of personal contact, and with the increased usage of email, it can create an atmosphere of misunderstandings and confused communications.

Poorly worded or carelessly read emails lead to unclear expectations, which can lead to more mistakes and increase the time spent on a task. Most of us (because of time constraints) don't take the time to ask for clarification; we just do it and hope for the best. (With uncertainty about how our performance is being viewed).

Given that most employees feel overworked, pushed too hard and not recognized for their contributions, the question remains: are they fulfilling their potential in the work place?

What do we do about it?

One thing is certain, there is no one answer. It is up to each of us to begin to look at what we are doing and ask ourselves the question "Is what I am doing working for me"?

If the answer is yes then continue to do it, but if the answer is no, it is time to begin to look at some new behaviors and what it is that you can begin to do differently.

Desire could be another word for motivation. If there is no desire then you will not change what you are doing. This is for people who desire to do things differently. Everything that we do in life becomes a habit, we do it because we have always done it this way and even though we don't like it, we continue to do it.

We are in a comfort zone and it may be painful, but we are used to it and we would rather stay with what we know then move into what we do not. Most of us are frightened of the unknown. We choose to stay in the familiar.

When you remove a behavior then you must replace it with a new behavior or you will revert back to the familiar.

Each of us knows what we are doing or not doing; we know everything about ourselves that we choose to know. The problem is we don't know how to change. Today we are going to craft out new behaviors for ourselves to bring about that change. In order to do this we need to gather our tools:

Tools for time mastery

1. **Commitment** is the first and the most important tool because without it there will be no change. The definition of commitment is when the action matches the word. Do not concern yourself with how you are going to do it; instead as the NIKE commercial says "Just do it"!
2. Knowing how to **prioritize** is next. It is a skill and as with any skill it can be learned. It is a very simple procedure and it must be done on a daily basis.
3. **Setting boundaries** and knowing how to say no are third. This is the most difficult tool but with practice you can train yourself to do it.
4. **Flexibility**, coming out of your comfort zone, and doing new actions is next.
5. Lastly, **possessing the knowledge and belief that you are worth it** will help you succeed.

There is a vast difference between wanting and doing.

➢ Wanting is waiting—It may come but chances are pretty good that it won't and nothing will change.
➢ Doing is "I can and I will" and is supplemented with action.

Attitudes and Beliefs

> ➢ What you think, you will create.
> ➢ If you think you can't, you won't.
> ➢ If you believe you can, you will.

Thoughts are powerful and they create. Reality is created from inside of you. Whatever is going on inside of you is happening on the outside. In order to change the outside you must begin to change the inside first. Change your thoughts; start paying attention to your self-talk. If it is not what you desire, change it immediately. Powerlessness is the most negative belief. It feels as though you are in a box without windows and doors, and that is not true. You can put in windows and doors!

Delegation

What is delegation and how do you do it?

It's simply assigning a task for another individual (or groups of individuals) to do. This is a skill which sounds easy but is not always exercised effectively.

Some delegate a task with little or no direction and hope that it gets completed in the way they would accomplish it. Others refuse to delegate at all; they are a one man band and consequently have work life issues.

There is a way to do it effectively. One critical ingredient that must be present in delegation is self-confidence and the ability to trust oneself. Without it the person will never be an effective delegator.

Trusting oneself, and ones choices, are key to delegating correctly. What is behind delegation is choosing the right person to do the job. Once you believe in yourself and possess a sense that you understand the strengths of others, the rest is easy.

EXERCISE 3.1—Delegation

1. On a scale of 1-5, how do you rate your delegation skills? (One being low and 5 being an effective).

2. How do you currently keep track of the task you have delegated? Is there a process?

3. In the future how do you plan to track delegated assignments? Are there any changes that you would like to make? If yes, what?

4. What do you do when you discover you made a mistake with your decision? Do you "live with it" because there is no one else to assume ownership for the task?

5. In the future how do you plan to learn from your mistakes? What could you do you differently?

EXERCISE 3.2—Time Constraints and Having Boundaries

1. Write an experience in which you recently were asked to do a task and said no.

2. What was the reason you said no and how did the person accept your answer? Were you comfortable with your answer, or would you have liked to go back and changed your response?

3. Do you have clearly defined boundaries for yourself? If the answer is yes, have you been able to communicate them to others or is it just for you? Why?

4. Do you know your priorities? Are they in order and clear for you or are they constantly shifting and moving around? What method are you currently using to form your priorities? Are they outside of your scope? (Ex. work, leader, fire alarms)? Are your priorities different at home then at work? Why?

5. Make a list of your top 3 priorities in order of importance to you (the first being the most important). Are you honoring this list? Why/why not?

6. Please provide your definition of **priorities** and **boundaries**. How do they differ? Which do you honor most?

7. How do you handle distractions and interruptions? Do you have a specific process or do you respond and react?

EXERCISE 3.3—Work/Life Balance

1. Define what "work life balance" means to you.

2. What is the first thing you want to change for yourself? (Do not consider how "doable" it is).

3. What actions are needed to achieve this goal? List at least 3 actions.

4. When and how are you going to take action? Get specific; supply a date and time.

5. What support system do you need to help you achieve your goal?

6. What metric will you use to know if you are making progress?

7. What will you do if this plan is not working for you? List alternative actions you can do.

8. How can you make this (and keep it) a priority for yourself?

Remember, in picking out a goal, Rome was not built in a day and you are not going to recreate yourself in one day either. This is about taking baby steps, not leaps. Everything starts with one step. A baby doesn't get up and run. In order to walk the baby is supported under both arms and takes shaky tentative steps in the beginning. Let's start with one step at a time.

Session 4—Mastering The Change Curve

Objectives

1. Refresher on the Change Curve.
2. Gain an understanding of the phases of change.
3. Pinpoint which stage you (and your team) are in.
4. Inspire yourself and your team to meet change head on.
5. Develop a strategy to master change.
6. Feel calmer and more in control.
7. View change as a need to grow vs. being an obstacle.
8. Identify behaviors that will help you move through the phases of change.

Innovative Approaches to Managing Change

Wouldn't it be beneficial to accept the challenges of changing rather than resist it?

Principles of change

1. Change is an ongoing process rather than an event.

2. There is a progressive sequence of change behaviors that needs to be experienced and mastered to be effective in handling change.

3. Seemingly negative behaviors such as denial, apprehension, anger and resistance are normal and adaptive elements in the change process.

4. There are specific strategies available to increase change mastery.

5. The progression through the phases of change represents an opportunity for growth and responsible risk taking.

"An effective change leader does not try to resolve people's feelings, but listens to them.

When leaders listen, acknowledge, and support people experiencing their difficult feelings, they will themselves begin to move through them".

Drs. Dennis Jaffe & **Cynthia Scott**

(Experts in change management)

Understanding Change

1. Defining involuntary and voluntary CHANGE
2. Understanding the negative and positive responses to change
3. Identifying your feelings, emotions and actions when change occurs
4. Learn how your preferred style impacts how you transition through change

When our expectations are significantly disrupted, the end-result is resistance.
The way we show our resistance differs on how we view the change.

Leadership and Change

It doesn't matter whether a change is originally seen as positive or negative; when people's expectations are significantly disrupted, the end result is resistance.

Negative Response to Change

There are **8 distinct stages** through which people pass whenever they feel trapped in a change they don't want and can't control.

Phase 1—Stability:
This phase precedes the announcement of the change. It represents the present state.

Phase 2—Immobilization:
This initial reaction is shock. Reactions may vary from temporary confusion to complete disorientation. The impact of change is so alien to the person's frame of reference that he/she is unable to relate to what is happening.

Phase 3—Denial:
The individual is unable to assimilate new information. Change related information is often rejected or ignored. Common reactions are "It won't happen to me", or "If I ignore it, it will go away."

Phase 4—Anger:
This phase is characterized by frustration and hurt, often manifested by indiscriminate lashing out. These emotions are often directed at friends and family, typically the ones most likely to be supportive.

Phase 5—Bargaining:
Here people begin negotiating to avoid the negative impact of change. Examples could be "I'll do it, but I need a deadline extension", or "I'd like to be reassigned." This marks the beginning of acceptance.

Phase 6—Depression:

This is represented by feelings of victimization and helplessness, resignation to failure and disengagement from one's work. At this point, the full weight of the negative change is finally acknowledged.

Phase 7—Testing:

People regain a sense of control by acknowledging the new limitations, but exploring ways to redefine goals.

Phase 8—Acceptance:

Individuals respond to change more realistically, but still may not like it.

Nevertheless, the price of a valued team member's not being able to complete the sequence can be even more costly. When someone gets stuck at or more of the phases, dysfunctional behavior typically escalates and can eat up an inordinate amount of time and energy for all concerned.

Positive Response to Change

People can also exhibit resistance to changes, which are normally considered positive. Think about getting married, having a baby, or getting a new job. There are **5 distinct phases** of positive resistance to change.

Phase 1—Uniformed optimism:

This is an overly idealistic perception of what is coming. Generally, the individual does not have a good picture of what the change will entail. They have a naïve enthusiasm based on insufficient data.

Phase 2—Informed pessimism:

Reality hits! As the change unfolds, we realize that what we expected does not happen and much (for which the person is not prepared) begins to take place. Public and/or private checking out may occur. This represents a withdrawal from the entire change process. "Checking out" manifests itself by either publicly displaying overt behavior, or by privately going underground and becoming detached. Public checking out is less destructive since there is an acknowledgement of problems.

Phase 3—Hopeful realism:

Beginning to see the light at the end of the tunnel. As more concerns are resolved, you become increasingly confident.

Phase 4—Informed optimism:

Individuals realize optimism based on a realization of the true situation. Successful experiences are frequently realized.

Phase 5—Completion:

This is the end to the process of change where new behaviors and attitudes are integrated within the person.

Working with team members and displaying a positive response to change may help. Keep in mind that all change is expensive; you either pay for what you want or you pay for not getting what you want, but you will always pay.

Positive and negative responses to change are adapted from Connor, D. (1993). **Managing At the Speed of Change**.

Mastering the Change Curve

Discussion points:
- The pace of change is increasing.
- Today's changes are broader in scope and more complex than in the past.
- Everyone looks at change in a different way.

Purpose
- To help you discuss, understand, and better adapt to change.

Denial
- Begins with the awareness of change.
- Is a defense against change; preserves the present.
- Takes the form of ignoring or not responding to information about the change.

Resistance
- A normal and natural reaction to change.
- Is a result of making people let go of their comfort zones.
- Why leave what is safe and comfortable?

Exploration
- Begins when the change is accepted.
- Involves feeling stronger and more proactive about making the change work.
- Less anxiety about the change and more confidence about taking the needed action.

Commitment
- Characterized by seeing the change as the "new norm".
- Feelings of success are a result of learning new skills and integrating the change into one's life.

Summary
- Change is a journey.
- Denial, Resistance, Exploration, and Commitment are normal, natural responses to change.
- There is no quick fix.
- Communication is key!

EXERCISE 4.1—Mastering the Change Curve Instrument

DENIAL

- Why is this change inconvenient, or why do you wish it were not happening?

- Does your behavior indicate that you think change will not happen? Are you not doing things that you could do to get ready?

- What will be the consequences to you if you do not change?

- What can you do, right now, to get ready for change?

RESISTANCE

- Why are you uncomfortable with what is happening right now?

- What are your greatest concerns about the future?

- What is the worst thing that could happen? How likely is this?

- What will be most difficult for you to achieve in this change?

EXPLORATION

- What do you have to learn? What new skills and behaviors do you need?

- What help do you need from people around you?

- What is the most positive vision you have of how the change can be successful?

- What do you have to stop doing in order to succeed in the new situation?

COMMITMENT

- What do you have to celebrate?

- What have you mastered?

- What areas do you still have to work on in order to continue to improve?

The Changing Nature of Change

- The pace of change is increasing.

- Today's changes are broader in scope and more complex than in the past.

- Everyone looks at change in a different way.

Change, Stress, and Trust

How individuals are impacted . . .

The pace of change is rapidly increasing and frequently creates stress. As organizations go through change, there are many affects. The usual way of doing things, including people's expectations about their jobs, are now in question. Clarity is being replaced with uncertainty; no one knows the final outcome and this is unsettling for many.

Change also breeds a climate of mistrust and suspicion. People don't know where they stand. Rumors fly and valid information is scarce. People don't know who they can trust. They worry about the outcome and feel like it is every man and woman for him-or-herself. Work can come to a standstill.

Responsiveness to change is also dependent on past experiences with change. What appears to be a big deal for one person may not be such a big deal for another. Change is both a challenge and an opportunity for growth. During any change there will be a period of adjustment in which anxiety and uncertainty increase. This period is accompanied by a corresponding decrease in efficiency and performance.

What techniques are appropriate to use with your team members who are in different phases of the negative change model? Another way to look at this, is to ask how you are planning on dealing with change? How will you communicate it? What methods will you use?

CHANGE PHASES	TECHNIQUES
Stability	
Immobilization	
Denial	
Anger	
Bargaining	
Depression	
Testing	
Acceptance	

EXERCISE 4.2—Techniques for handling change

So, as a leader, what could you do to handle change with your team members? Think of the models presented above. Consider the following questions and record your answers for discussion.

- What recent change has happened in your organization or in your personal life?

- Where do you fit in the model, and what can you do for yourself?

- What should you look for in your team members? Where in the model do they fit? What can you do to help them?

Session 5—Trust

Objectives

1. Obtain a deeper understanding of trust
2. Assess levels of trust and how we express it
3. Learn strategies for giving and receiving empowering feedback
4. Identify behaviors that indicate that trust exists between individuals
5. Learn the major factors that influence the decision to trust or not to trust

Trust is the underlying foundation of practically every human transaction. It makes it possible to collaborate with each other and achieve collective results. It affects our relationships at home, work, and in our communities.

Like financial wealth, it takes time and effort to accumulate and build trust, and if it is lost or betrayed it can be very difficult to regain. Although, we use the word frequently, very few of us know the actually meaning of the word. It is almost impossible to clearly define. What we do understand is the importance of the word to us, and our constant question to ourselves "can I trust this person"?

Trust produces positive and productive relationships. When trust exists, communication is open, conflicts can be addressed in a healthy manner, and collaboration is enhanced because of sharing resources and jointly solving problems. In other words, it becomes easier to work together when it is present. Lack of trust occurs over time and reversing the process takes even longer.

"Trust has become ever more important because it helps us manage complexity, fosters a capacity for action, enhances collaboration, and increases organizational learning". (Robert Shaw, Trust in the Balance: Building Successful Organizations on Result, Integrity, and Concern, 1997, p 17)

__Definitions of Trust__

1. Trust is ultimately what allows leaders to lead. (Craig Weatherup in Shaw, 1997)
2. Teamwork relies on its interdependency. Team members must rely on one another to achieve their goals. (Kinlaw, 1991)
3. Trust is the basis of these relationship that span organizational boundaries.
4. Trust allows operating efficiencies because the need to control and monitor is reduced. It becomes associated with a high performing workplace (Shaw 1997)
5. Trust enables people of all levels to have more latitude in doing what is required to win in the market place
6. Trust takes the place of supervision because direct supervision of employees becomes impractical (Mayer, Davis, and Schoorman 1995)

Intentions behind trust

Do we believe that individuals act out of self-interest or for the greater good for service?

If we believe that we act out of self-interest, we put measures in to control and restrict behavior so that it will contribute to the greater good.

If we believe that we act for the greater good, our behavior will not be restricted and we will have greater freedom.

According to Hosmer, 1995 *"just the word trust evokes powerful emotions that can appear to be irrational"*

More definitions of trust

- Blind trust is when someone trusts without considering the risks involved. (Mayer et al, 1995)
- Total confidence that the person will carry out the depended-on action. Trust is based in part on faith. (Shaw 1997)
- Predictability that the person will behave in a predictable manner
- Mechanical cooperation that the motives go beyond the role requirements to serve the best interest of the trustor.

There are four distinct characteristics of trust based on the learnings of Mayer et al, and HRDQ

1. Evidence of lack of Monitoring
2. Evidence of Benevolence
3. Evidence of Openness
4. Evidence of Risk-Taking

Trust is not limited to how we view other people; it is also about trusting oneself and our choices. In leadership one of the major components is delegation. Most people who have trouble delegating are faced with trusting themselves and their competencies for selecting the right person for the task. Delegation is a skill that can be learned and improved. The first step is to believe that you have the capability to select the perfect person for the job. In other words it begins with you.

Here are some questions that can be utilized in the selection process for your "perfect delegate". This person:

1. Has successfully completed a similar task
2. Has failed and performed poorly on a similar task
3. Has the education or training to necessary to perform this task
4. Has shown an aptitude for this sort of task
5. Has not shown an aptitude for this task
6. Came through for me or someone I know
7. Let me down
8. Broke a promise or commitment
9. Taken an action inconsistent with his or her spoken beliefs
10. Taken an action that I found surprising based on what I know of him or her
11. Said one thing and done something else
12. Done what he or she said they would
13. Broken a confidence
14. Kept a confidence
15. Confided in me or opened up to me
16. Withheld information from me

Asking oneself these questions at the beginning of the selection process will allow you to have more clarity about the candidates that you are thinking about selecting. There is no one sure method, but clarity is essential in the selection of the right candidate.

People trust those who consider their interests even in the face of potentially conflicting pressures. Commitment is an essential factor of trust. In the face of adversity, having someone sticking to their guns and standing up for what they believe in allows people to believe that the person will do what he feels is right and inspires trust and loyalty in others. (Robert Shaw, Tough Trust: A Conversation with Craig Weatherup of Pepsico, Leader to Leader, 1997, p50)

When we trust someone we do not worry about restricting the flow of information to them. We will reveal our true selves; even aspects that may be unflattering. We will also contribute ideas, interests or prospects.

Of the several variables that affect trust, one by far has the greatest impact. It is that you care. Love and caring are the most powerful of human emotions in terms of their positive effect on trust in relationships. This is true in the workplace and in all relationships (Bill Maynard, Heart and Soul, and Spirit: Bold Strategies for Transforming Your Organization, 1996, p51)

In contrast, when we don't feel trust we limit the information we reveal about ourselves and only give flattering, vague or very little personal data. We fear the information will be used against us. We are <u>not</u> willing to take a risk.

We also rely on rules and put controls in place to check that the untrusting behavior is acceptable. Per Frey, 1993 (a prominent economist) "feelings of being distrusted can bring a response of a lack of work effort. When we trust someone we undertake actions that benefit the person without immediately expecting something in return".

EXERCISE 5.1—TO TRUST OR NOT TO TRUST . . .

Each of us has the ability to choose to trust or not to trust. The range includes absolute unwillingness to trust to the extreme willingness to trust everything. This range of levels of trust may cause conflicts in both personal and professional relationships.

1. On a scale of 1-5 (1 not trusting at all and 5 trusting everyone and everything) what is your current level of trust? (at work).

1   2   3   4   5

2. Would you like to increase or decrease your level? Why?

3. Think of a relationship where trust exists. What did that individual do to have you trust him/her?

4. What was the result for you? Did it work? Why?

5. What is the one behavior that someone must display for you to begin to trust them?

6. Have you ever lost trust in someone? If yes, was it more difficult for you to rebuild trust?

<u>**Characteristics that will engender trust**</u> (according to Drucker, 1997 and Sinetar, 1988)

> - *Integrity*—Does this person act in accordance with his/her stated beliefs?
> - *Predictability*—Do you have a good idea how this person will act in any given situation?
> - *Reliability*—Can you count on them to keep their promises? Is there follow through?
> - *Benevolence*—Do they act in a way that honors their relationship with you, when you are not present?

We find it easier to trust someone we share similarities with (ex. generational, religious, and political) and tend to think the more someone is like us the more we can trust them.

When one person has greater power or influence over another person, trust can be difficult to achieve. Feeling vulnerable to the person in a position of power is a greater risk than usual. The person in power also has problems trusting because the person feels compelled to do so. When there is a sense of competition it is difficult to achieve trust within the relationship. According to Marsha Sinetar, 1988 this is called "the one winner mentality". This can happen within any relationship.

<u>**Feedback and Trust**</u>

There are many factors that figure in our decision to trust someone. Some include:

> - Our individual tendency to trust
> - Our history and experience with this person
> - How a person carries out commitments
> - How similar or different we are with the individual
> - Our relative power and authority
> - Our work environment
> - Our experience over time with an individual
> - The person's relationship with us and with others important to us

Feedback is a difficult situation as it impacts both the giver and receiver. In feedback, it is important not to impart to the person receiving the feedback a bashing, and punishing experience. It is of major importance to focus on their strengths as well as what is not working for them.

Behaviors make us who we are. We need to assess what isn't working as it is most likely linked to a strength that is either being overused or underused!

When feedback is done in a positive, honoring way, it allows the receiver to take control of their behavior with a sense of empowerment and one of being in control. The level of trust the receiver has for the giver directly impacts what they may or may not do about what they have heard.

The higher the level of trust the higher the tendency to take action on the information they have been given. When you have seen a behavior change, it is important to tell the person that you have noticed the change. Rewards, recognition and consequences are needed ingredients for the experience to work.

Guidelines for Giving (and getting) Feedback

1. Explain the intention of the session and stress the anonymity that what is communicated will not leave the room.
2. Don't beat around the bush.
3. Don't pass judgment.
4. Describe the behavior and how it affects you.
5. Share exactly how it makes you feel.
6. Don't play amateur psychologist.
7. Listen with an open mind.
8. Don't get defensive.
9. Separate yourself from your behavior.
10. Check the fit; be honest with yourself. Does it ring true?

EXERCISE 5.2—TRUST and FEEDBACK

1. Identify the team member you have the most interaction with. How do you get along with this person?

2. Why is your relationship working or not working with them?

3. Have you been able to give this person constructive feedback? Why?

4. Have they given you constructive feedback?

5. Did you feel honored during the feedback process?

EXERCISE 5.3—TRUST and RELATIONSHIPS

1. How have individual team member's tendencies to trust affected the development of trust within the team? What are some of the advantages of a group composed of members who tend to trust? What are some of the potential pitfalls?

2. How have similarities and differences among individual members affected the development of trust in the team? What could you do to uncover similarities?

3. How have members' previous experiences with one another, either as individuals or within a group, affected the level of trust in this team or group?

4   How have differences in power or authority among individual members affected the development of trust in this team or group?

5. How has the organizational environment encouraged or discouraged the development of trust in this team or group?

6. What evidence of trust or distrust do you observe in the behavior of team members?

Trust according to Webster's dictionary is: ***Reliance on the integrity, strength, and ability of a person or thing; inspire confidence***

EXERCISE 5.4—TRUST and COMMUNICATION

1. Define the word trust using your own definition.

2. Name some attributes that someone you have trusted has displayed.

3. How has this impacted how you communicate with one another?

4. What was the impact of working with someone that you did not trust? (a peer, leader, business partner?).

5. What could your leader change to improve the levels of trust you have with him/her?

Ways to build trust

1. Act with integrity; walk the talk (Marsha Sinetar, 1988) Our motives and behaviors must be understandable. The person who says one thing but believes another is unpredictable and will not inspire trust

2. Protect the interest of people who are not present. (Peterson & Hicks, 1997) If someone is absent from a meeting or a discussion, take the responsibility of presenting their point of view.

3. Listen. (Warren Bennis,1996) One of the best ways to build deep trust is by deep listening. It is the most powerful dynamic of human interaction when people feel they are being heard.

4. Be sensitive and respectful. (Marsha Sinetar,1988) People will not open up to those who lack empathy, are quick to judge, or laugh or make jokes when someone is speaking seriously.

5. Take the leap. (1997 interview with Craig Weatherup, Chairman and CEO of Pepsico) observed that trust always requires someone to go first (Shaw, 1997) It can be a simple gesture such as giving someone your home phone number.

6. Make realistic commitments and keep them. (Petersen & Hicks, 1997) Over-promising and under-delivering is a sure way to erode trust.

7. Judge substance, not image (Sinetar, 1988) When we make assumptions about others beliefs abilities and character based upon outside issues such as appearance we may later find out that we were wrong.

8. Offer status reports and forecasts. (Petersen & Hooks, 1997) Keep others informed of future plans. They will be less likely to check up on you since you provide them with consistent and timely updates and information.

Session 6—Interpersonal Influence Inventory
How You Come Across To Others . . . .

Objectives

1. Learn your style of influencing others
2. Become familiar with four influencing styles and indicators
3. Identify areas of strength and areas for improvement
4. Apply newly learned skills on the job and at home

Why we are here?

To explore the factors which influence our styles and behaviors. As individuals, we are most influenced by:
*   Past experiences
*   Attitudes and beliefs
*   Self-confidence

We will also review three types of learning as defined by HRDQ's instrument *"Interpersonal Influence Inventory"*:
*   Associative
    When an individual associates a behavior without even thinking about it.

*   Reinforcement
    When an individual learns the consequences from their actions such as rewards or punishments.

*   Modeling
    When an individual learns the consequences of behavior by watching someone else perform the action.

Situation:

As Zuker (1983) points out, the internal dialogue we have with ourselves greatly influences our behavior. Fears inhibit us from expressing our opinions, especially when we fear rejection.

Another major inhibitor is the guilt of saying no. People feel an intense desire to please which conflicts with saying "no", or "not now".

In order to stand up for oneself it is important for the person to feel self-worth and a sense of value. If self-esteem is not present within the person, the act of taking care of oneself is also not present.

Without self-confidence one will not be able to demonstrate assertive behavior. (Kelly, 1979)

Assertiveness and expression go hand and hand. The skill of communication is about making choices for oneself. If a person is not likely to express themselves, their achievement of their goals are less likely as well.

Being assertive allows the individual the opportunity to be able to control the situation because they are able to communicate their feelings. Others involved in the situation are more at ease because of the information that has been transmitted.

> ➤ Assertiveness usually leads to a win-win situation. It leads to a balance of power because the information maximizes the rights of all powers

Styles and Behaviors to Understand

Alberti (1977) defines assertiveness as:

> "*Behavior that enables a person to act in his or her own best interest,*
> *to stand up for him or herself without undue anxiety,*
> *to express his or her honest feelings comfortably,*
> *or to exercise his or her own rights without denying the rights of others*".

- Assertiveness is a characteristic of behavior and not a person.
- Assertiveness is a collection of skills that can be learned.
- Assertiveness is person and situation specific; there are particular situations in which a behavior is more likely to occur.
- Assertive behavior is in the eye of the beholder. Diverse cultures will view the behavior differently.
- Assertiveness is the ability of the individual to choose his or her actions instead of being constrained by a situation.
- Assertive behavior is not aimed at getting one's way or intended to harm others in order to fulfill one's own desires.

➢ There are two different styles that are used in influencing others:

1. Openness in communication
2. Consideration for others

Openness in communication—

A person is open to sharing their life experiences, thoughts and emotions with others.

The opposing style prefers to volunteer very little information about oneself.

Consideration for others—

An individual's willingness to accord others the same rights that he wants for him/herself. They are people who will fight to preserve the rights of others as they do their own.

The opposing style is to have little respect for the opinions, feelings, and reactions of others.

In communication there are four distinct indicators that are communicated:

1. Thoughts
2. Emotions
3. Nonverbal behavior
4. Verbal behavior

These behaviors are communicated both directly and indirectly.

FOUR INFLUENCE STYLES

➢ ASSERTIVE BEHAVIOR:
Having self-confidence and a belief that everyone has rights. Their desires should not be denied or pursued at the expense of others.

Emotions
Individuals are even tempered. Anger or frustration that is felt is recognized and controlled directed at the situation not the people.

Nonverbal behavior
Upright comfortable posture, direct eye contact, and appropriate tone of voice.

Verbal behavior
Clear, concise and direct. Individuals speak in the first person. They directly express their views and desire to have alternative viewpoints.

➢ PASSIVE BEHAVIOR:

<u>Thoughts</u>
Has the belief that they should not speak their minds, either because they have no confidence in themselves or they are afraid to disturb the relationship. They do not like to disagree, and believe that they are inadequate and that others have rights but they do not.

<u>Emotions</u>
Hiding one's feelings from others; feels depressed and victimized. Anger and resentment are held inside and this can sometimes blow up unexpectedly.

<u>Nonverbal behavior</u>
Slumped posture, downcast eyes, nervous gestures.

<u>Verbal behavior</u>
Uses qualifiers such as "I am probably wrong but, if it is OK with you"; speaks in a weak voice or stilted speech.

➢ CONCEALED AGGRESSIVE BEHAVIOR

<u>Thoughts</u>
Hostile thoughts, concealed about getting back at the person in a devious manner.

<u>Emotions</u>
Hostility, anger and tension.

<u>Nonverbal Behavior</u>
Rigid posture, glaring eye contact. Behavior is icy and controlled.

<u>Verbal Behavior</u>
Insults and threats but aimed indirectly at others such as gossip. There is no full expression of anger but it is felt; gossip and sabotage are likely.

➢ OPENLY AGGRESSIVE BEHAVIOR

<u>Thoughts</u>
Believe they have rights but others do not. They feel they should always be in control and they are never wrong. Worry only about themselves, are not afraid of hurting others.

<u>Emotions</u>
Anger, hostility and resentment. Feels the world is against them; they are stressed and feel frustrated.

<u>Nonverbal Behavior</u>
A fighting stance in the body. Glares at others; rigid and tense posture; point and shake their fist.

<u>Verbal behavior</u>
Speak in loud and haughty tone of voice. They can be insulting and make derogatory comments. Verbal abuse is common. This involves direct, forceful and rude interactions with others.

EXERCISE 6.1—Effective Listening

Answer each question using the rating scale of 1-5 (5 being best). Don't be afraid to use 5!

Please be as honest as you can be; your answers are confidential and will not be shared with the class or the instructor unless you choose to

Listening skill is more than half for determining your effectiveness in communication. Verbal and nonverbal are also part of communication, and sometimes the message that is not spoken is just as effective (or ineffective) as words . . .

SCORE 1-5

1. Am I an effective listener?   _____

2. Do I interrupt someone when they are slow to get to the point?   _____

3. Do I give my undivided attention to the person who is speaking to me?   _____

4. Do I make and keep eye contact throughout the conversation if not why?   _____

5. Am I aware of the tone of voice I am using when I am interested in the
    conversation and when I am not.   _____

6. How aware am I of my facial expressions and my posture?   _____

7. Are my verbal communications clear and direct when I am uncomfortable?   _____

8. Am I more at ease having general conversations, rather than business?   _____

9. Do I contribute in meetings when my opinion does not agree with
    the majority?   _____

10. Do I feel part of the team?   _____

11. What is the one area from these questions that you would like to improve?   _____

Our Behaviors

Behaviors are learned as a child and we continue to display them throughout the years unless we make a conscious decision to change them or deviate from them.

It is difficult for someone who demonstrates passive behavioral traits to feel safe and stand up for themselves and what they believe in. Most times those that practice the descriptions explained above don't want to rock the boat even though they might feel strongly about their beliefs; the habit of the behavior will win out!

Influencing without authority can be such a case. How does one influence without authority? Can it be achieved? Does it work? Let's look at it.

Passion has a lot to do with what a person is willing to do to influence others. Without passion in what one believes, it is so much easier to just let majority rule and go along with everyone else. When passion exists, the individual is much more likely to influence others to the best of their ability and take the risk of stepping out of their comfort zone. Revealing your passion when your opinion may be in the minority is a risk, but a risk worth taking.

Influencing without authority can be difficult. This can be especially true when you are asked to do a task and it causes conflict with your beliefs and what you are passionate about.

Doing what is in your heart is important to you, but can differ from what you are requested to do.

When differences occur:

- The first step is to remove emotion from the situation.
- Next is to objectively review your priorities
    o How much internal conflict does this cause me?
    o How important is this job to me?
    o Do I clearly understand the value and need for the task?
- How can I motivate myself and then others to accomplish the task?
- What consequences am I willing to accept if I choose not to support the task?

The person I need to influence most in these situations is me!

Behaviors and Conflict

Conflict is everywhere. It exists within every interpersonal relationship whether it be at home, work, or play. The definition of conflict according to the Thomas-Kilmann Conflict instrument is: "a difference of opinion by two or more people". Conflict is a part of life; it involves our attitudes, and includes how we are perceived.

The concealed behavior is sometimes more difficult to detect than the openly aggressive behavior. Let's discover if this is really the case.

Have you ever had the experience that you were angry and made up your mind that you weren't going to show it? Everyone kept coming over to you asking the same questions: "are you okay? You seem angry? I hope I haven't done anything to make you angry!"

As you grit your teeth you responded: "no, I am not angry at all". This did nothing but escalate the anger and the situation. Usually the other person will get angry as well, because they detect the response is insincere and don't appreciate it. It is always best to be honest and indicate that something is amiss, but there is no need to explain why unless you choose to. Most conflicts are resolved by telling the truth and listening to what the other person has to say without the emotion of needing to be right or justifying and rationalizing it.

People striving toward a common goal find solutions. Think in terms of:
1. What do we need to have happen in this meeting?
2. What do we have to do to get there?
3. What must I leave this room with clarity about?

One's goals and objectives must be present for each party to achieve an equitable solution. Resolving conflicts may appear easier when one is in a position of authority, but resolution may also be attained without "pulling rank" by searching for that common goal.

INFLUENCE SKILLS

a) BODY POSTURE
b) FACIAL EXPRESSION
c) EYE CONTACT
d) TONE OF VOICE
e) FLUENCY OF SPEECH
f) DIRECTNESS OF SPEECH
g) VERBAL BEHAVIOR

EXERCISE 6.2—Acquired Skills

1. What skills have you learned from this session?

2. What was the most difficult form of communication for you, verbal or nonverbal?

3. How will you apply your new found skill in your daily communications?

4. Identify one new behavior that you will begin to use immediately:

5. Name a behavior from another person that prompts a reaction from you?

6. How does self-confidence influence you, and what were your thoughts about the influencing style you used?

EXERCISE 6.3—Influencing Your Business Partner

You are a member of a ten person team. The team consists of a leader, a technical lead, a project manager and 7 technicians. The team has been given a project that must be completed within a thirty day time frame. This will be impossible unless the funding is increased.

You have been designated to influence the business partner to increase the funding for the team. The business partner has a reputation of being a tough nut to crack.

The entire well being of the team rests with you and your assertiveness.

> ➢ How will you influence the business partner to see things your way?

> ➢ The business partner is openly aggressive and believes that only their rights are important; they are very low on the scale of consideration for others.

One person will be observing your technique in achieving your goal, and the other person will play the role of the business partner.

The observer will take notes on the following:

1) Body posture

2) Facial expression

3) Eye contact

4) Tone of voice

5) Fluency of speech

6) Directness of speech

7) Verbal behavior

Prior to role playing jot down some behaviors you would like to display and some key phrases and points that will help you achieve your goal:

How did you feel? Did you achieve your goal?

Session 7—Coping With Stress

Objectives

1. Obtain a better understanding of stress; learn to recognize it and how to cope with it.
2. Measure your stress levels.
3. Create a personal plan for effective stress management techniques.
4. Learn how to take charge of your stress and not let it overwhelm you.
5. Identify what you can do differently to maintain your balance during times of high levels of stress.

For this session you will be guided through a series of self-discoveries and learn tools that will position you to be **motivated by potentially stressful situations, instead of being negatively impacted.**

Why we are here?

Stress usually brings a negative assumption to individuals. Most of us are so used to being stressed that we don't even realize that we are. That is when our body lets us know it is having problems. There are people that totally shut down when experiencing stress and others that go into "overdrive". What may potentially cause one person to shut down may be another's gift or inspiration.

Depression is also an internal reaction to high levels of stress and although the body is able to handle it, over time it will wear down the body and its immune system and physical symptoms will occur.

Physical symptoms of stress may include:

➤ headaches
➤ backaches
➤ feeling tired and lacking energy
➤ a generally feeling of not being well

What can we do?

The first step in handling stress is to be aware of it. Without awareness, stress is in control of you and not the other way around. Even when you are aware, the questions remain:
"What am I going to do about it"?
"How do I cope with my stress"?

With probably the most important question being:
"Is what I am doing working"?

The Concise Oxford Dictionary tells us that stress is "*A constraining or impelling force of effort, demand, upon physical or mental energy.*" This view construes stress as a stimulus—something that is external to the individual, group or organization. In this context stress has been defined as:

a) mental fatigue
b) role ambiguity
c) unusual demand
d) stressful situation
e) overload/underload
f) stimulation overload
g) unpredictability of future events
h) role conflict
i) role overload
j) role strain
k) situational stress

Think of stress like a bank account. You can keep drawing out of your account as long as you continue to make deposits. If you exclusively withdraw (with no further deposits), you will eventually deplete your account and go into the red because you will have used up all of your reserves.

In spite of the importance of stress, there is little coherence in theory, and research reflects no agreed upon terminology. Some people may use the word stress and others may use anxiety, conflict, and frustration. (Lazarus, 1966, p.2, emphasis added)

Two types of job stress may threaten the employee:
1. Job demands, which the employee may or may not be able to master or successfully counter
2. Insufficient supplies or support in the work place

We must accept that stress in the workplace exists and work to understand what it means.

Our interpretations of the definitions of stress inform or misinform us about what stress is and what it is not. Definitions of stress have led to controversy and misunderstandings about the nature of stress and range from simple to comprehensive and complex.

Stress may be a stimulus, a response, or a relationship between the environment and the person. It is also an umbrella term under which a wide range of issues and human functions and work performance can be understood and managed.

EXERCISE 7.1—Place a check mark after you quickly read each question:

	(in the past)				
Symptoms of stress:	right now	3 mos	6mos	9 mos	12 mos
1. Do you feel tense?	_____	_____	_____	_____	_____
2. Do you feel tired?	_____	_____	_____	_____	_____
3. Are you depressed?	_____	_____	_____	_____	_____
4. Have you lost your confidence?	_____	_____	_____	_____	_____
5. Do you get angry easily?	_____	_____	_____	_____	_____
6. Do you have bad indigestion?	_____	_____	_____	_____	_____
7. Are you nervous?	_____	_____	_____	_____	_____
8. Do you have cramps?	_____	_____	_____	_____	_____
9. Do you have ulcers?	_____	_____	_____	_____	_____
10. Does your mouth feel dry?	_____	_____	_____	_____	_____
11. Do you get pains in your chest?	_____	_____	_____	_____	_____
12. Do you sweat too much?	_____	_____	_____	_____	_____
13. Do you get too many headaches?	_____	_____	_____	_____	_____
14. Is your thinking sometimes unclear?	_____	_____	_____	_____	_____
15. Do you sometimes feel dizzy or faint?	_____	_____	_____	_____	_____
16. Do you get upset for no reason?	_____	_____	_____	_____	_____
17. Is it difficult to sleep properly?	_____	_____	_____	_____	_____
18. Have you lost interest in others?	_____	_____	_____	_____	_____
19. Do you have trouble concentrating?	_____	_____	_____	_____	_____
20. Is decision-making a problem?	_____	_____	_____	_____	_____

Seekers guide to stress

Balance is the key to managing stress. If the employee is over stimulated or under stimulated, the effects will adversely affect the employee's job performance. We are in an information age where the rate of which workers have to face and respond to information has multiplied exponentially. We are immersed in information over load.

How we manage this avalanche of information constitutes one of the biggest causes of stress we face today. Time is the biggest enemy for employees. The issue is that the rapid flow of information is outstripping our capacity to manage the time available. Studying employees in large corporations found that e-mails received and sent averaged 178 messages a day and was usually interrupted by new messages three or more times an hour, each one supposedly urgent. The cumulative effect of the message deluge is chronic distractedness (Coleman, 1999, p76)

When we are bombarded with too many stimuli demands (messages), our response system weakens and we no longer function at capacity with our reactions less crisp.

The pace of change not only outpaces the employee's capacity to be productive and impacts their relationships with co-workers, but it also begins to affect their personal relationships and lifestyle.

People need to feel good about themselves. We are measured by our external achievements and no matter how involved or supportive our parents may have been, no matter how much they built us up and tried to make us feel great about ourselves, it is virtually impossible for us to escape the framework of success set up by society. (Jeffers, 1995, pp6-7)

The need to <u>achieve</u> is a natural drive; it is learned throughout life and reflected in the way children are brought up and socialized into the adult values of the prevailing culture.

The need to compete and the drive for competition is threaded throughout our lives. We validate ourselves and our success by whether we have won or lost. We feel bad about ourselves when we don't meet our own expectations and that impacts our lives; the thin line of work/ life balance begins to shift and we become off balanced trying to do better and win more competitions.

In fact we tend to make everything in our lives a competition and therefore, we never relax or let go, we just keep reducing our energy bank until there is nothing left to take out.

Stress is often linked to disease

Stress and the **G**eneral **A**daption **S**yndrome (GAS)

Seyle developed the GAS syndrome and the 3 stage process

➤ Stage 1   Alarm Shock phase. Physical or mental demands that a person begins to feel responses from the body; raised heartbeat, body temperature.

➤ Stage 2   Resistance phase. A marked decrease in the individual's capacity to deal with other demands that require attention.

➤ Stage 3   Exhaustion phase. Stressor is continuous and severe; taxes what is left of the person's capacity for adapting. This can be followed by life threatening illness.

EXERCISE 7.2—Stress in the Workplace

Situation:

Mid-level manager; open office. An employee is allocated to a new work team. The team leader repeatedly bullies and picks on the employee causing him to feel threatened.

When not at work, the employee feels miserable and anxious and thinks about the next time(s) he will have to face this particular person. To complicate matters even more, the employee's family has worked in the company and he has been told not to let them down.

They also stated they will have nothing to do with him if he does not make a good impression.

1. As the manager, what would you do with the employee in this situation?

2. What could you do to get the employee to share what (s)he is feeling?

3. Is there anything that you would do to help lower the level of stress for the employee and for yourself, what?

4. Have you ever been faced with a similar situation and if you have what did you do? Did it work? Would you do something else today?

Stress Damage: The cost to industry and individuals

It is estimated that the workplace stress epidemic in the USA is costing over $150 billion a year. As early as 1984, the Control Data Corporation analyzed the medical claims of their employees and discovered that on the average an unhealthy employee cost the company $509 more annually then a healthy one. They also found that there was a 5% higher absenteeism rate.

Side note: Replacing a manager at work who is underperforming because of stress can cost up to 90 % of their replacements first year salary.

Surveys conducted by D'Arcy, Masius, Benton and Bowles indicate 75% of American employees say their jobs cause them stress; the Employment Gazette recently claimed that of 328 million absences, 111 million (just under a third) were associated with stress.

Stress is an employee and a work place problem.

Stress management options such as systematic relaxation, meditation, massage and access to exercise facilities as well as stress management seminars offered significant benefits to employees.

Because of our different personalities, some of us seek out stress related situations because of the high need for stimulation. There are also some who need to have a high degree of predictability in their life. The people who have high need for stimulation take more risks.

Stress management solutions are inspired by critical thinkers. Critical thinking is a knowledge tool to promote improvements and benefit everyone.

Role demands

Role demands imposed by employers are intended to ensure that the tasks of the organization are carried out efficiently and effectively. Employees designated as carrying out particular roles are regarded as being the role occupant.

In studies of stress at work, the main problems for role occupants are found in role conflict, role ambiguity, role load and role responsibility for others. Role demands on employees can engender so much role strain that they under-perform at work.

> ➤ Role Demands:
>   Are clearly defined tasks, performances and behavior expected from the role occupant?
> ➤ Role Ambiguity:
>   Uncertain nature of the tasks to be performed and the competencies and behaviors needed to carry that role increases the level of stress of the employee.

➢ Role Responsibility:
    Individual carries too much responsibility for managing and supervising other people at work. They are not given enough training and their level of stress will increase.

➢ Role conflict:
    Mixed messages are given as to what is expected of them and how they should go about performing their roles at work.

➢ Role load
    A measure of the complete range of roles in carrying out a job as well as personal roles.

Clarity of roles and matching skill sets with job requirements will help minimize stress. Remember the adage "*Hire hard or manage hard*".

EXERCISE 7.3—What Causes You Stress?

1. What has to happen for you not to feel stressed? Is this dependent on someone else's actions or your own?

2. What motivates you to action? Circle all that apply to you (you can add to the list if you desire).

Calm	Clarity	Others:
Stress	Confusion	
Chaos	Boundary encroachment	
Decisiveness	Exhaustion	
Indecisiveness	Money	
Passion	Worry	
Needs	Conflict	
Consequences	Time Constraints	

After you have circled all that apply, identify the one which impacts you the greatest. Explain why.

3. Am I able to tell what others need from me? How? List 3 ways without using verbal communication by actions only.

    a. _____

    b. _____

    c. _____

4. List 3 of your needs that can be met by others.

    a. _____

    b. _____

    c. _____

5. How could you meet these needs yourself? What actions would you need to do?

6. Would you hire you in your present position?

Describe 2 demanding situations where you cope very well and experience little or no stress:

Description:

    1.

    2.

Coping strategies:

    1.

    2

How did you minimize/eliminate the stress symptoms?

    1.

    2.

How can these coping strategies be leveraged for other demanding situations?

EXERCISE 7.4—Stress in Our Organization

1. How do you view stress in your organization?

2. Do team members really deal with the stress problem? How?

3. Is the method of managing stress at work working, and for whom is it working?

4. What are the valid sources of stress at work?

5. Are attempts being made to improve management of stress in the work place?

6. How appropriate is the level of stress management intervention?

7. Are you satisfied with the evaluation of stress problems in the work place?

8. How critical are we in adapting a particular approach to managing stress management?

9. What criteria could we adopt to judge the success or failure of stress management initiatives?

Session 8—Case Study

Objectives

1. To discuss what the 'barriers' are that are coming up for you and preventing you from achieving all that you desire.
2. To lay the groundwork for each of you to create a Case Study to link the concepts that you are applying from Leadership Journey II (and Leadership Journey I where applicable) to *Move Beyond your Barriers*.

Session 9—Wrap-Up—Putting It All Together

Objectives

1. Recap learnings
2. Present Case Studies
3. Compare/Discuss pre-post scores
4. Discuss if your expectations have been met
5. Review areas of improvement and areas to track
6. Graduation!

Congratulations! You have completed *PeopleTek's Leadership Journey® II—Moving Beyond The Barriers* program. Here you will have the opportunity to reflect on what you have learned in your continuing journey for leadership excellence and to commit to making specific behavioral changes.

You will complete the "Where Are You Now" exercise that was initially completed in session 1 and compare your results. This allows you to recap all that you have learned during our time together and plan for future travels. You should keep it close to you so that it can serve as a daily reminder of your strengths and your ideas for continuing your leadership development.

Pre/Post Discussion

➢ Have your scores changed since the beginning of the journey?
   If yes, how? If not, why do you think you've remained constant?

_____

_____

_____

➢ What actions have you done to initiate the change? Are there any other actions you plan to do to support the changes you'd like to make?

_____

_____

_____

_____

We wish you the best as your *Journey* continues!

About The Author

Michael W. Kublin is the founder and President of PeopleTek, Inc, a leadership coaching and development company specializing in helping leaders, teams, and organizations thrive by having the courage and commitment to lead with a purpose, implement strategies and plans, and communicate with confidence and clarity.

PeopleTek specializes in enabling leaders of all levels, and their teams, to examine their behaviors and determine what is/is not effective and to identify what may be inhibiting desired results.

Since 1996, PeopleTek is credited with helping thousands of individuals and businesses improve their efficiency and effectiveness while increasing personal and corporate satisfaction. By examining behaviors, leveraging preferred styles, and by removing fear from leadership, organizational growth occurs and results improve.

In 1999 Michael took his knowledge and developed the comprehensive 12 session leadership program, *LEADERSHIP JOURNEY I*, to provide attendees with the processes to enhance their leadership skills and abilities. In 2007, Mike and his PeopleTek team developed *Leadership Journey II* (exclusively for Leadership Journey I graduates). Its focus is on removing barriers that impede success, the application of leadership business concepts, and the creation of comprehensive individual action plans that support skill development and strategies for organizational improvement.

Prior to founding PeopleTek, Mike worked for Electronic Data Systems and American Express in a variety of leadership roles managing technical teams and interfacing with internal and external business partners and vendors.

Mike received his undergraduate degree from the University of Florida, and his MBA from Nova Southeastern University. He's author of <u>12 Steps For Courageous Leadership</u>, is on the Graduate School Advisory Board for Keiser University, on the Board of Directors for non-profit Catch 81, is ITIL v 3 certified, and is a member of SHRM and ICF.

Journey II—At a Glance

Instrument *Indicate your profile results below*	Awareness and Future Actions *What have you learned from your preferred style?* *What could you change to enhance your style?*
WORK EXPECTATIONS High > Low >	
MASTERING THE CHANGE CURVE Denial: Resistance: Exploration: Commitment:	
COMMUNICATION STYLES Direct: Spirited: Systematic: Considerate:	
TRUST Low Mod High Lack Of Monitoring: Benevolence: Openness: Risk-Taking:	

Instrument *Indicate your profile results below*	Awareness and Future Actions *What have you learned from your preferred style?* *What could you change to enhance your style?*

INTERPERSONAL INFLUENCE INV
                 VL   L   Avg   H   VH
  Assertive
  Passive
  Concealed
    Aggressive
  Openly
    Aggressive	

COPING and STRESS
                 VL   L   Mod   H   VH
Personal Profile:
  Stress:
  Problem Solving:
  Communication:
  Closeness:
  Flexibility:
  Satisfaction:
Work Profile:
  Stress:
  Problem Solving:
  Communication:
  Closeness:
  Flexibility:
  Satisfaction:	

Instrument	Awareness and Future Actions
Indicate your profile results below	*What have you learned from your preferred style?* *What could you change to enhance your style?*
TIME MASTERY Level **I II III IV V** Attitudes: Goals: Priorities: Analyzing: Planning: Scheduling: Interruptions: Meetings: Written Communication: Delegation: Procrastination: Team Time:	

What actions/behaviors do you want to leave behind?

List new actions you commit to while continuing on your *Journey* through Leadership.